Heaven and Earth by Lord Byron

A MYSTERY. PART I

George Gordon Byron, 6th Baron Byron, but more commonly known as just Byron was a leading English poet in the Romantic Movement along with Keats and Shelley.

Byron was born on January 22nd, 1788. He was a great traveller across Europe, spending many years in Italy and much time in Greece. With his aristocratic indulgences, flamboyant style along with his debts, and a string of lovers he was the constant talk of society.

In 1823 he joined the Greeks in their war of Independence against the Ottoman Empire, both helping to fund and advise on the war's conduct.

It was an extraordinary adventure, even by his own standards. But, for us, it is his poetry for which he is mainly remembered even though it is difficult to see where he had time to write his works of immense beauty. But write them he did.

He died on April 19th 1824 after having contracted a cold which, on the advice of his doctors, was treated with blood-letting. This cause complications and a violent fever set in. Byron died like his fellow romantics, tragically young and on some foreign field.

Index of Contents

"And it came to pass … that the sons of God saw the daughters of men that they were fair; and they took them wives of all which they chose."

"And woman wailing for her demon lover."

Coleridge.

DRAMATIS PERSONÆ
ANGELS
Samiasa
Azaziel

Raphael
The Archangel
Noah and his Sons
Irad
Japhet
Anah
Aholibamah
Chorus of Spirits of the Earth
Chorus of Mortals

PART I

Scene I

—A woody and mountainous district near Mount Ararat.

—Time, midnight.

Enter ANAH and AHOLIBAMAH.

ANAH - Our father sleeps: it is the hour when they
Who love us are accustomed to descend
Through the deep clouds o'er rocky Ararat:—
How my heart beats!

AHOLIBAMAH - Let us proceed upon
Our invocation.

ANAH - But the stars are hidden.
I tremble.

AHOLIBAMAH - So do I, but not with fear
Of aught save their delay.

ANAH - My sister, though
I love Azaziel more than—oh, too much!
What was I going to say? my heart grows impious.

AHOLIBAMAH - And where is the impiety of loving
Celestial natures?

ANAH - But, Aholibamah,
I love our God less since his angel loved me:
This cannot be of good; and though I know not
That I do wrong, I feel a thousand fears
Which are not ominous of right.

AHOLIBAMAH - Then wed thee
Unto some son of clay, and toil and spin!
There's Japhet loves thee well, hath loved thee long:
Marry, and bring forth dust!

ANAH - I should have loved
Azaziel not less were he mortal; yet
I am glad he is not. I cannot outlive him.
And when I think that his immortal wings
Will one day hover o'er the sepulchre
Of the poor child of clay which so adored him,
As he adores the Highest, death becomes
Less terrible; but yet I pity him:
His grief will be of ages, or at least
Mine would be such for him, were I the Seraph,
And he the perishable.

AHOLIBAMAH - Rather say,
That he will single forth some other daughter
Of earth, and love her as he once loved Anah.

ANAH - And if it should be so, and she loved him,
Better thus than that he should weep for me.

AHOLIBAMAH - If I thought thus of Samiasa's love,
All Seraph as he is, I'd spurn him from me.
But to our invocation!—'Tis the hour.

ANAH - Seraph!
From thy sphere!
Whatever star contain thy glory;
In the eternal depths of heaven
Albeit thou watchest with "the seven,"
Though through space infinite and hoary
Before thy bright wings worlds be driven,
Yet hear!
Oh! think of her who holds thee dear!
And though she nothing is to thee,
Yet think that thou art all to her.
Thou canst not tell,—and never be
Such pangs decreed to aught save me,—
The bitterness of tears.
Eternity is in thine years,
Unborn, undying beauty in thine eyes;
With me thou canst not sympathise,
Except in love, and there thou must
Acknowledge that more loving dust
Ne'er wept beneath the skies.
Thou walk'st thy many worlds, thou see'st
The face of him who made thee great,

As he hath made me of the least
Of those cast out from Eden's gate:
Yet, Seraph dear!
Oh hear!
For thou hast loved me, and I would not die
Until I know what I must die in knowing,
That thou forget'st in thine eternity
Her whose heart Death could not keep from o'er-flowing
For thee, immortal essence as thou art!
Great is their love who love in sin and fear;
And such, I feel, are waging in my heart
A war unworthy: to an Adamite
Forgive, my Seraph! that such thoughts appear,
For sorrow is our element;
Delight
An Eden kept afar from sight,
Though sometimes with our visions blent.
The hour is near
Which tells me we are not abandoned quite. —
Appear! Appear!
Seraph!
My own Azaziel! be but here,
And leave the stars to their own light!

AHOLIBAMAH - Samiasa!
Wheresoe'er
Thou rulest in the upper air—
Or warring with the spirits who may dare
Dispute with him
Who made all empires, empire; or recalling
Some wandering star, which shoots through the abyss,
Whose tenants dying, while their world is falling,
Share the dim destiny of clay in this;
Or joining with the inferior cherubim,
Thou deignest to partake their hymn—
Samiasa!
I call thee, I await thee, and I love thee.
Many may worship thee, that will I not:
If that thy spirit down to mine may move thee,
Descend and share my lot!
Though I be formed of clay,
And thou of beams
More bright than those of day
On Eden's streams,
Thine immortality can not repay
With love more warm than mine
My love. There is a ray
In me, which, though forbidden yet to shine,
I feel was lighted at thy God's and thine.
It may be hidden long: death and decay
Our mother Eve bequeathed us—but my heart

Defies it: though this life must pass away,
Is that a cause for thee and me to part?
Thou art immortal—so am I: I feel—
I feel my immortality o'ersweep
All pains, all tears, all fears, and peal,
Like the eternal thunders of the deep,
Into my ears this truth—"Thou liv'st for ever!"
But if it be in joy
I know not, nor would know;
That secret rests with the Almighty giver,
Who folds in clouds the fonts of bliss and woe.
But thee and me he never can destroy;
Change us he may, but not o'erwhelm; we are
Of as eternal essence, and must war

With him if he will war with us; with thee
I can share all things, even immortal sorrow;
For thou hast ventured to share life with me,
And shall
I shrink from thine eternity?
No! though the serpent's sting should pierce me thorough,
And thou thyself wert like the serpent, coil
Around me still! and I will smile,
And curse thee not; but hold
Thee in as warm a fold
As — but descend, and prove
A mortal's love
For an immortal. If the skies contain
More joy than thou canst give and take, remain!

ANAH - Sister! sister! I view them winging
Their bright way through the parted night.

AHOLIBAMAH - The clouds from off their pinions flinging,
As though they bore to-morrow's light.

ANAH - But if our father see the sight!

AHOLIBAMAH - He would but deem it was the moon
Rising unto some sorcerer's tune
An hour too soon.

ANAH - They come! He comes!—Azaziel!

AHOLIBAMAH - Haste
To meet them! Oh! for wings to bear
My spirit, while they hover there,
To Samiasa's breast!

ANAH - Lo! they have kindled all the west,
Like a returning sunset;—lo!

On Ararat's late secret crest
A mild and many-coloured bow,
The remnant of their flashing path,
Now shines! and now, behold! it hath
Returned to night, as rippling foam,
Which the Leviathan hath lashed
From his unfathomable home,
When sporting on the face of the calm deep,
Subsides soon after he again hath dashed
Down, down, to where the Ocean's fountains sleep.

AHOLIBAMAH - They have touched earth! Samiasa!

ANAH - My Azaziel!

[Exeunt.

Scene II.

—Enter IRAD and JAPHET.

IRAD - Despond not: wherefore wilt thou wander thus
To add thy silence to the silent night,
And lift thy tearful eye unto the stars?
They cannot aid thee.

JAPHET - But they soothe me—now
Perhaps she looks upon them as I look.
Methinks a being that is beautiful
Becometh more so as it looks on beauty,
The eternal beauty of undying things.
Oh, Anah!

IRAD - But she loves thee not.

JAPHET - Alas!

IRAD - And proud Aholibamah spurns me also.

JAPHET - I feel for thee too.

IRAD - Let her keep her pride,
Mine hath enabled me to bear her scorn:
It may be, time too will avenge it.

JAPHET - Canst thou
Find joy in such a thought?

IRAD - Nor joy nor sorrow.

I loved her well; I would have loved her better,
Had love been met with love: as 'tis, I leave her
To brighter destinies, if so she deems them.

JAPHET - What destinies?

IRAD - I have some cause to think
She loves another.

JAPHET - Anah!

IRAD - No; her sister.

JAPHET - What other?

IRAD - That I know not; but her air,
If not her words, tells me she loves another.

JAPHET - Aye, but not Anah: she but loves her God.

IRAD - Whate'er she loveth, so she loves thee not,
What can it profit thee?

JAPHET - True, nothing; but
I love.

IRAD - And so did I.

JAPHET - And now thou lov'st not,
Or think'st thou lov'st not, art thou happier?

IRAD - Yes.

JAPHET - I pity thee.

IRAD - Me! why?

JAPHET - For being happy,
Deprived of that which makes my misery.

IRAD - I take thy taunt as part of thy distemper,
And would not feel as thou dost for more shekels
Than all our father's herds would bring, if weighed
Against the metal of the sons of Cain—
The yellow dust they try to barter with us,
As if such useless and discoloured trash,
The refuse of the earth, could be received
For milk, and wool, and flesh, and fruits, and all
Our flocks and wilderness afford.—Go, Japhet,
Sigh to the stars, as wolves howl to the moon—
I must back to my rest.

JAPHET - And so would I
If I could rest.

IRAD - Thou wilt not to our tents then?

JAPHET - No, Irad; I will to the cavern, whose
Mouth they say opens from the internal world,

To let the inner spirits of the earth
Forth when they walk its surface.

IRAD - Wherefore so?
What wouldst thou there?

JAPHET - Soothe further my sad spirit
With gloom as sad: it is a hopeless spot,
And I am hopeless.

IRAD - But 'tis dangerous;
Strange sounds and sights have peopled it with terrors.
I must go with thee.

JAPHET - Irad, no; believe me
I feel no evil thought, and fear no evil.

IRAD - But evil things will be thy foe the more
As not being of them: turn thy steps aside,
Or let mine be with thine.

JAPHET - No, neither, Irad;
I must proceed alone.

IRAD -
Then peace be with thee!

[Exit IRAD.-

JAPHET - (solus).
Peace! I have sought it where it should be found,
In love—with love, too, which perhaps deserved it;
And, in its stead, a heaviness of heart,
A weakness of the spirit, listless days,
And nights inexorable to sweet sleep
Have come upon me. Peace! what peace? the calm
Of desolation, and the stillness of
The untrodden forest, only broken by
The sweeping tempest through its groaning boughs;
Such is the sullen or the fitful state
Of my mind overworn. The Earth's grown wicked,
And many signs and portents have proclaimed

A change at hand, and an o'erwhelming doom
To perishable beings. Oh, my Anah!
When the dread hour denounced shall open wide
The fountains of the deep, how mightest thou
Have lain within this bosom, folded from
The elements; this bosom, which in vain
Hath beat for thee, and then will beat more vainly,
While thine—Oh, God! at least remit to her
Thy wrath! for she is pure amidst the failing

As a star in the clouds, which cannot quench,
Although they obscure it for an hour. My Anah!
How would I have adored thee, but thou wouldst not;
And still would I redeem thee—see thee live
When Ocean is earth's grave, and, unopposed
By rock or shallow, the Leviathan,
Lord of the shoreless sea and watery world,
Shall wonder at his boundlessness of realm.

[Exit JAPHET.

Enter NOAH and SHEM -

NOAH - Where is thy brother Japhet?

SHEM - He went forth,
According to his wont, to meet with Irad,
He said; but, as I fear, to bend his steps
Towards Anah's tents, round which he hovers nightly,
Like a dove round and round its pillaged nest;
Or else he walks the wild up to the cavern
Which opens to the heart of Ararat.

NOAH - What doth he there? It is an evil spot
Upon an earth all evil; for things worse
Than even wicked men resort there: he
Still loves this daughter of a fated race,
Although he could not wed her if she loved him,
And that she doth not. Oh, the unhappy hearts
Of men! that one of my blood, knowing well
The destiny and evil of these days,
And that the hour approacheth, should indulge
In such forbidden yearnings! Lead the way;
He must be sought for!
SHEM - Go not forward, father:
I will seek Japhet.
NOAH - Do not fear for me:
All evil things are powerless on the man
Selected by Jehovah.—Let us on.

SHEM - To the tents of the father of the sisters?

NOAH - No; to the cavern of the Caucasus.

[Exeunt NOAH and SHEM.-

Scene III.

—The mountains.—A cavern, and the rocks if Caucasus.

JAPHET - (solus).
Ye wilds, that look eternal; and thou cave,
Which seem'st unfathomable; and ye mountains,
So varied and so terrible in beauty;
Here, in your rugged majesty of rocks
And toppling trees that twine their roots with stone
In perpendicular places, where the foot
Of man would tremble, could he reach them—yes,
Ye look eternal! Yet, in a few days,
Perhaps even hours, ye will be changed, rent, hurled
Before the mass of waters; and yon cave,
Which seems to lead into a lower world,
Shall have its depths searched by the sweeping wave,
And dolphins gambol in the lion's den!
And man — Oh, men! my fellow-beings! Who
Shall weep above your universal grave,
Save I? Who shall be left to weep? My kinsmen,
Alas! what am I better than ye are,
That I must live beyond ye? Where shall be
The pleasant places where I thought of Anah
While I had hope? or the more savage haunts,
Scarce less beloved, where I despaired for her?
And can it be!—Shall yon exulting peak,
Whose glittering top is like a distant star,
Lie low beneath the boiling of the deep?
No more to have the morning sun break forth,
And scatter back the mists in floating folds
From its tremendous brow? no more to have
Day's broad orb drop behind its head at even,
Leaving it with a crown of many hues?
No more to be the beacon of the world,
For angels to alight on, as the spot
Nearest the stars? And can those words "no more"
Be meant for thee, for all things, save for us,
And the predestined creeping things reserved
By my sire to Jehovah's bidding? May
He preserve them, and I not have the power
To snatch the loveliest of earth's daughters from
A doom which even some serpent, with his mate,

Shall 'scape to save his kind to be prolonged,
To hiss and sting through some emerging world,
Reeking and dank from out the slime, whose ooze
Shall slumber o'er the wreck of this, until
The salt morass subside into a sphere
Beneath the sun, and be the monument,
The sole and undistinguished sepulchre,
Of yet quick myriads of all life? How much
Breath will be stilled at once! All beauteous world!
So young, so marked out for destruction, I
With a cleft heart look on thee day by day,
And night by night, thy numbered days and nights.
I cannot save thee, cannot save even her
Whose love had made me love thee more; but as
A portion of thy dust, I cannot think
Upon thy coming doom without a feeling
Such as—Oh God! and canst thou—

[He pauses.

[A rushing sound from the cavern is heard, and shouts of laughter—afterwards a SPIRIT passes.

JAPHET - In the name
Of the Most High, what art thou?

SPIRIT - (laughs).
Ha! ha! ha!

JAPHET -
By all that earth holds holiest, speak!

SPIRIT - (laughs).
Ha! ha!

JAPHET - By the approaching deluge! by the earth
Which will be strangled by the ocean! by
The deep which will lay open all her fountains!
The heaven which will convert her clouds to seas,
And the Omnipotent who makes and crushes!
Thou unknown, terrible, and indistinct,
Yet awful Thing of Shadows, speak to me!
Why dost thou laugh that horrid laugh?

SPIRIT - Why weep'st thou?

JAPHET - For earth and all her children.

SPIRIT - Ha! ha! ha!

[SPIRIT vanishes.

JAPHET - How the fiend mocks the tortures of a world,
The coming desolation of an orb,
On which the sun shall rise and warm no life!
How the earth sleeps! and all that in it is
Sleep too upon the very eve of death!
Why should they wake to meet it? What are here,
Which look like death in life, and speak like things
Born ere this dying world? They come like clouds!

[Various SPIRITS pass from the cavern.

SPIRIT - Rejoice!
The abhorréd race
Which could not keep in Eden their high place,
But listened to the voice
Of knowledge without power,
Are nigh the hour,
Of Death!
Not slow, not single, not by sword, nor sorrow,
Nor years, nor heart-break, nor Time's sapping motion,

Shall they drop off. Behold their last to-morrow!
Earth shall be Ocean!
And no breath,
Save of the winds, be on the unbounded wave!
Angels shall tire their wings, but find no spot:
Not even a rock from out the liquid grave
Shall lift its point to save,
Or show the place where strong Despair hath died,
After long looking o'er the ocean wide
For the expected ebb which cometh not:
All shall be void,
Destroyed!
Another element shall be the lord
Of life, and the abhorred
Children of dust be quenched; and of each hue
Of earth nought left but the unbroken blue;
And of the variegated mountain
Shall nought remain
Unchanged, or of the level plain;
Cedar and pine shall lift their tops in vain:
All merged within the universal fountain,
Man, earth, and fire, shall die,
And sea and sky
Look vast and lifeless in the eternal eye.
Upon the foam
Who shall erect a home?

JAPHET - (coming forward).
My sire!
Earth's seed shall not expire;

Only the evil shall be put away
From day.
Avaunt! ye exulting demons of the waste!
Who howl your hideous joy
When God destroys whom you dare not destroy:
Hence! haste!
Back to your inner caves!
Until the waves
Shall search you in your secret place,

And drive your sullen race
Forth, to be rolled upon the tossing winds,
In restless wretchedness along all space!

SPIRIT - Son of the saved!
When thou and thine have braved
The wide and warring element;
When the great barrier of the deep is rent,
Shall thou and thine be good or happy?—No!
Thy new world and new race shall be of woe—
Less goodly in their aspect, in their years
Less than the glorious giants, who
Yet walk the world in pride,
The Sons of Heaven by many a mortal bride.
Thine shall be nothing of the past, save tears!
And art thou not ashamed
Thus to survive,
And eat, and drink, and wive?
With a base heart so far subdued and tamed,
As even to hear this wide destruction named,
Without such grief and courage, as should rather
Bid thee await the world-dissolving wave,
Than seek a shelter with thy favoured father,
And build thy city o'er the drowned earth's grave?
Who would outlive their kind,
Except the base and blind?
Mine
Hateth thine
As of a different order in the sphere,
But not our own.
There is not one who hath not left a throne
Vacant in heaven to dwell in darkness here,
Rather than see his mates endure alone.
Go, wretch! and give
A life like thine to other wretches—live!
And when the annihilating waters roar
Above what they have done,
Envy the giant patriarchs then no more,
And scorn thy sire as the surviving one!
Thyself for being his son!

Chorus of SPIRITS issuing from the cavern.
Rejoice!
No more the human voice
Shall vex our joys in middle air
With prayer;
No more
Shall they adore;
And we, who ne'er for ages have adored
The prayer-exacting Lord,
To whom the omission of a sacrifice
Is vice;
We, we shall view the deep's salt sources poured
Until one element shall do the work
Of all in chaos; until they,
The creatures proud of their poor clay,
Shall perish, and their bleached bones shall lurk
In caves, in dens, in clefts of mountains, where
The deep shall follow to their latest lair;
Where even the brutes, in their despair,
Shall cease to prey on man and on each other,
And the striped tiger shall lie down to die
Beside the lamb, as though he were his brother;
Till all things shall be as they were,
Silent and uncreated, save the sky:
While a brief truce
Is made with Death, who shall forbear
The little remnant of the past creation,
To generate new nations for his use;
This remnant, floating o'er the undulation
Of the subsiding deluge, from its slime,
When the hot sun hath baked the reeking soil
Into a world, shall give again to Time
New beings—years, diseases, sorrow, crime—
With all companionship of hate and toil,
Unitl—

JAPHET - (interrupting them).
The eternal Will
Shall deign to expound this dream
Of good and evil; and redeem
Unto himself all times, all things;
And, gathered under his almighty wings,

Abolish Hell!
And to the expiated Earth
Restore the beauty of her birth,
Her Eden in an endless paradise,
Where man no more can fall as once he fell,
And even the very demons shall do well!

SPIRIT - And when shall take effect this wondrous spell?

JAPHET - When the Redeemer cometh; first in pain,
And then in glory.

SPIRIT - Meantime still struggle in the mortal chain,
Till Earth wax hoary;
War with yourselves, and Hell, and Heaven, in vain,
Until the clouds look gory
With the blood reeking from each battle-plain;
New times, new climes, new arts, new men; but still,
The same old tears, old crimes, and oldest ill,
Shall be amongst your race in different forms;
But the same moral storms
Shall oversweep the future, as the waves
In a few hours the glorious giants' graves.

Chorus of SPIRITS - Brethren, rejoice!
Mortal, farewell!
Hark! hark! already we can hear the voice
Of growing Ocean's gloomy swell;
The winds, too, plume their piercing wings;
The clouds have nearly filled their springs;
The fountains of the great deep shall be broken,
And heaven set wide her windows; while mankind
View, unacknowledged, each tremendous token—
Still, as they were from the beginning, blind.
We hear the sound they cannot hear,
The mustering thunders of the threatening sphere;
Yet a few hours their coming is delayed;

Their flashing banners, folded still on high,
Yet undisplayed,
Save to the Spirit's all-pervading eye.
Howl! howl! oh Earth!
Thy death is nearer than thy recent birth;
Tremble, ye mountains, soon to shrink below
The Ocean's overflow!
The wave shall break upon your cliffs; and shells,
The little shells, of ocean's least things be
Deposed where now the eagle's offspring dwells—
How shall he shriek o'er the remorseless sea!
And call his nestlings up with fruitless yell,
Unanswered, save by the encroaching swell;—
While man shall long in vain for his broad wings,
The wings which could not save:—
Where could he rest them, while the whole space brings
Nought to his eye beyond the deep, his grave?
Brethren, rejoice!
And loudly lift each superhuman voice—
All die,
Save the slight remnant of Seth's seed—

The seed of Seth,
Exempt for future sorrow's sake from death.
But of the sons of Cain
None shall remain;
And all his goodly daughters
Must lie beneath the desolating waters;
Or, floating upward, with their long hair laid
Along the wave, the cruel heaven upbraid,
Which would not spare
Beings even in death so fair.
It is decreed,
All die!
And to the universal human cry
The universal silence shall succeed!
Fly, brethren, fly!
But still rejoice!
We fell!

They fall!
So perish all
These petty foes of Heaven who shrink from Hell!

[The SPIRITS disappear, soaring upwards.

JAPHET - (solus).
God hath proclaimed the destiny of earth;
My father's ark of safety hath announced it;
The very demons shriek it from their caves;
The scroll of Enoch prophesied it long
In silent books, which, in their silence, say
More to the mind than thunder to the ear:
And yet men listened not, nor listen; but
Walk darkling to their doom: which, though so nigh,
Shakes them no more in their dim disbelief,
Than their last cries shall shake the Almighty purpose,
Or deaf obedient Ocean, which fulfils it.
No sign yet hangs its banner in the air;
The clouds are few, and of their wonted texture;
The Sun will rise upon the Earth's last day
As on the fourth day of creation, when
God said unto him, "Shine!" and he broke forth
Into the dawn, which lighted not the yet
Unformed forefather of mankind—but roused
Before the human orison the earlier
Made and far sweeter voices of the birds,
Which in the open firmament of heaven
Have wings like angels, and like them salute
Heaven first each day before the Adamites:
Their matins now draw nigh—the east is kindling—
And they will sing! and day will break! Both near,
So near the awful close! For these must drop

Their outworn pinions on the deep; and day,
After the bright course of a few brief morrows,—
Aye, day will rise; but upon what?—a chaos,
Which was ere day; and which, renewed, makes Time
Nothing! for, without life, what are the hours?
No more to dust than is Eternity
Unto Jehovah, who created both.
Without him, even Eternity would be
A void: without man, Time, as made for man,
Dies with man, and is swallowed in that deep
Which has no fountain; as his race will be
Devoured by that which drowns his infant world.—
What have we here? Shapes of both earth and air?
No—all of heaven, they are so beautiful.
I cannot trace their features; but their forms,
How lovelily they move along the side
Of the grey mountain, scattering its mist!
And after the swart savage spirits, whose
Infernal immortality poured forth
Their impious hymn of triumph, they shall be
Welcome as Eden. It may be they come
To tell me the reprieve of our young world,
For which I have so often prayed.—They come!
Anah! oh, God! and with her—

Enter SAMIASA, AZAZIEL, ANAH, and AHOLIBAMAH.

ANAH - Japhet!

SAMIASA - Lo!
A son of Adam!

AZAZIEL - What doth the earth-born here,
While all his race are slumbering?

JAPHET - Angel! what
Dost thou on earth when thou should'st be on high?

AZAZIEL - Know'st thou not, or forget'st thou, that a part
Of our great function is to guard thine earth?

JAPHET - But all good angels have forsaken earth,
Which is condemned; nay, even the evil fly
The approaching chaos. Anah! Anah! my
In vain, and long, and still to be, beloved!
Why walk'st thou with this Spirit, in those hours
When no good Spirit longer lights below?

ANAH - Japhet, I cannot answer thee; yet, yet
Forgive me—

JAPHET - May the Heaven, which soon no more
Will pardon, do so! for thou art greatly tempted.

AHOLIBAMAH - Back to thy tents, insulting son of Noah!
We know thee not.

JAPHET - The hour may come when thou
May'st know me better; and thy sister know
Me still the same which I have ever been.

SAMIASA - Son of the patriarch, who hath ever been
Upright before his God, whate'er thy gifts,
And thy words seem of sorrow, mixed with wrath,
How have Azaziel, or myself, brought on thee
Wrong?

JAPHET - Wrong! the greatest of all wrongs! but, thou
Say'st well, though she be dust—I did not, could not,
Deserve her. Farewell, Anah! I have said
That word so often! but now say it, ne'er

To be repeated. Angel! or whate'er
Thou art, or must be soon, hast thou the power
To save this beautiful—these beautiful
Children of Cain?

AZAZIEL - From what?

JAPHET - And is it so,
That ye too know not? Angels! angels! ye
Have shared man's sin, and, it may be, now must
Partake his punishment; or, at the least,
My sorrow.

SAMIASA - Sorrow! I ne'er thought till now
To hear an Adamite speak riddles to me.

JAPHET - And hath not the Most High expounded them?
Then ye are lost as they are lost.

AHOLIBAMAH - So be it!
If they love as they are loved, they will not shrink
More to be mortal, than I would to dare
An immortality of agonies
With Samiasa!

ANAH - Sister! sister! speak not
Thus.

AZAZIEL - Fearest thou, my Anah?

ANAH - Yes, for thee:
I would resign the greater remnant of
This little life of mine, before one hour
Of thine eternity should know a pang.

JAPHET - It is for him, then! for the Seraph thou
Hast left me! That is nothing, if thou hast not
Left thy God too! for unions like to these,
Between a mortal and an immortal, cannot
Be happy or be hallowed. We are sent
Upon the earth to toil and die; and they
Are made to minister on high unto
The Highest: but if he can save thee, soon
The hour will come in which celestial aid
Alone can do so.

ANAH - Ah! he speaks of Death.

SAMIASA - Of death to us! and those who are with us!
But that the man seems full of sorrow, I
Could smile.

JAPHET - I grieve not for myself, nor fear.
I am safe, not for my own deserts, but those
Of a well-doing sire, who hath been found
Righteous enough to save his children. Would
His power was greater of redemption! or
That by exchanging my own life for hers,
Who could alone have made mine happy, she,
The last and loveliest of Cain's race, could share
The ark which shall receive a remnant of
The seed of Seth!

AHOLIBAMAH - And dost thou think that we,
With Cain's, the eldest born of Adam's, blood
Warm in our veins,—strong Cain! who was begotten
In Paradise,—would mingle with Seth's children?
Seth, the last offspring of old Adam's dotage?
No, not to save all Earth, were Earth in peril!
Our race hath always dwelt apart from thine
From the beginning, and shall do so ever.

JAPHET - I did not speak to thee, Aholibamah!
Too much of the forefather whom thou vauntest
Has come down in that haughty blood which springs
From him who shed the first, and that a brother's!
But thou, my Anah! let me call thee mine,
Albeit thou art not; 'tis a word I cannot
Part with, although I must from thee. My Anah!
Thou who dost rather make me dream that Abel
Had left a daughter, whose pure pious race

Survived in thee, so much unlike thou art
The rest of the stern Cainites, save in beauty,
For all of them are fairest in their favour—

AHOLIBAMAH - (interrupting him).
And would'st thou have her like our father's foe
In mind, in soul? If
I partook thy thought,
And dreamed that aught of
Abel was in her!—
Get thee hence, son of Noah; thou makest strife.

JAPHET - Offspring of Cain, thy father did so!

AHOLIBAMAH - But
He slew not Seth: and what hast thou to do
With other deeds between his God and him?

JAPHET - Thou speakest well: his God hath judged him, and
I had not named his deed, but that thyself
Didst seem to glory in him, nor to shrink
From what he had done.

AHOLIBAMAH - He was our father's father;
The eldest born of man, the strongest, bravest,
And most enduring:—Shall I blush for him
From whom we had our being? Look upon
Our race; behold their stature and their beauty,
Their courage, strength, and length of days—

JAPHET - They are numbered.

AHOLIBAMAH - Be it so! but while yet their hours endure,
I glory in my brethren and our fathers.

JAPHET - My sire and race but glory in their God,
Anah! and thou?—

ANAH - Whate'er our God decrees,
The God of Seth as Cain, I must obey,
And will endeavour patiently to obey.
But could I dare to pray in his dread hour
Of universal vengeance (if such should be),
It would not be to live, alone exempt
Of all my house. My sister! oh, my sister!
What were the world, or other worlds, or all
The brightest future, without the sweet past—
Thy love, my father's, all the life, and all
The things which sprang up with me, like the stars,
Making my dim existence radiant with
Soft lights which were not mine? Aholibamah!

Oh! if there should be mercy—seek it, find it:
I abhor Death, because that thou must die.

AHOLIBAMAH - What, hath this dreamer, with his father's ark,
The bugbear he hath built to scare the world,
Shaken my sister? Are we not the loved
Of Seraphs? and if we were not, must we
Cling to a son of Noah for our lives?
Rather than thus—But the enthusiast dreams
The worst of dreams, the fantasies engendered

By hopeless love and heated vigils. Who
Shall shake these solid mountains, this firm earth,
And bid those clouds and waters take a shape
Distinct from that which we and all our sires
Have seen them wear on their eternal way?
Who shall do this?

JAPHET - He whose one word produced them.

AHOLIBAMAH – Who heard that word?

JAPHET - The universe, which leaped
To life before it. Ah! smilest thou still in scorn?
Turn to thy Seraphs: if they attest it not,
They are none.

SAMIASA -
Aholibamah, own thy God!

AHOLIBAMAH - I have ever hailed our Maker, Samiasa,
As thine, and mine: a God of Love, not Sorrow.

JAPHET - Alas! what else is Love but Sorrow? Even
He who made earth in love had soon to grieve
Above its first and best inhabitants.

AHOLIBAMAH - 'Tis said so.

JAPHET - It is even so.

Enter NOAH and SHEM.

NOAH - Japhet! What
Dost thou here with these children of the wicked?
Dread'st thou not to partake their coming doom?

JAPHET - Father, it cannot be a sin to seek
To save an earth-born being; and behold,
These are not of the sinful, since they have
The fellowship of angels.

NOAH - These are they, then,
Who leave the throne of God, to take them wives
From out the race of Cain; the sons of Heaven,
Who seek Earth's daughters for their beauty?

AZAZIEL - Patriarch!
Thou hast said it.

NOAH - Woe, woe, woe to such communion!
Has not God made a barrier between Earth
And Heaven, and limited each, kind to kind?

SAMIASA - Was not man made in high Jehovah's image?
Did God not love what he had made? And what
Do we but imitate and emulate
His love unto created love?

NOAH - I am
But man, and was not made to judge mankind,
Far less the sons of God; but as our God
Has deigned to commune with me, and reveal
His judgments, I reply, that the descent
Of Seraphs from their everlasting seat
Unto a perishable and perishing,
Even on the very eve of perishing, world,
Cannot be good.

AZAZIEL - What! though it were to save?

NOAH - Not ye in all your glory can redeem
What he who made you glorious hath condemned.
Were your immortal mission safety, 'twould
Be general, not for two, though beautiful;
And beautiful they are, but not the less
Condemned.

JAPHET - Oh, father! say it not.

NOAH - Son! son!
If that thou wouldst avoid their doom, forget
That they exist: they soon shall cease to be,
While thou shalt be the sire of a new world,
And better.

JAPHET - Let me die with this , and
them!

NOAH – Thou shouldst for such a thought, but shalt not: he
Who can, redeems thee.

SAMIASA - And why him and thee,
More than what he, thy son, prefers to both?

NOAH - Ask him who made thee greater than myself
And mine, but not less subject to his own
Almightiness. And lo! his mildest and
Least to be tempted messenger appears!

Enter RAPHAEL the ARCHANGEL.

RAPHAEL - Spirits!
Whose seat is near the throne,
What do ye here?
Is thus a Seraph's duty to be shown,
Now that the hour is near
When Earth must be alone?
Return!
Adore and burn,
In glorious homage with the elected "Seven."
Your place is Heaven.

SAMIASA - Raphael!
The first and fairest of the sons of God,
How long hath this been law,
That Earth by angels must be left untrod?
Earth! which oft saw
Jehovah's footsteps not disdain her sod!
The world he loved, and made
For love; and oft have we obeyed
His frequent mission with delighted pinions:
Adoring him in his least works displayed;
Watching this youngest star of his dominions;
And, as the latest birth of his great word,
Eager to keep it worthy of our Lord.
Why is thy brow severe?
And wherefore speak'st thou of destruction near?

RAPHAEL - Had Samiasa and Azaziel been
In their true place, with the angelic choir,
Written in fire
They would have seen
Jehovah's late decree,
And not enquired their Maker's breath of me:
But ignorance must ever be
A part of sin;
And even the Spirits' knowledge shall grow less
As they wax proud within;
For Blindness is the first-born of Excess.
When all good angels left the world, ye stayed,
Stung with strange passions, and debased
By mortal feelings for a mortal maid:

But ye are pardoned thus far, and replaced

With your pure equals. Hence! away! away!
Or stay,
And lose Eternity by that delay!

AZAZIEL - And thou! if Earth be thus forbidden
In the decree
To us until this moment hidden,
Dost thou not err as we
In being here?

RAPHAEL - I came to call ye back to your fit sphere,
In the great name and at the word of God,
Dear, dearest in themselves, and scarce less dear—
That which I came to do: till now we trod
Together the eternal space; together
Let us still walk the stars. True, Earth must die!
Her race, returned into her womb, must wither,
And much which she inherits: but oh! why
Cannot this Earth be made, or be destroyed,
Without involving ever some vast void
In the immortal ranks? immortal still
In their immeasurable forfeiture.
Our brother Satan fell; his burning will
Rather than longer worship dared endure!
But ye who still are pure!
Seraphs! less mighty than that mightiest one,—
Think how he was undone!
And think if tempting man can compensate
For Heaven desired too late?
Long have I warred,
Long must I war
With him who deemed it hard
To be created, and to acknowledge him
Who midst the cherubim
Made him as suns to a dependent star,
Leaving the archangels at his right hand dim.
I loved him—beautiful he was: oh, Heaven!
Save his who made, what beauty and what power
Was ever like to Satan's! Would the hour
In which he fell could ever be forgiven!
The wish is impious: but, oh ye!
Yet undestroyed, be warned! Eternity
With him, or with his God, is in your choice:
He hath not tempted you; he cannot tempt
The angels, from his further snares exempt:
But man hath listened to his voice,
And ye to woman's—beautiful she is,
The serpent's voice less subtle than her kiss.
The snake but vanquished dust; but she will draw

A second host from heaven, to break Heaven's law.
Yet, yet, oh fly!
Ye cannot die;
But they
Shall pass away,
While ye shall fill with shrieks the upper sky
For perishable clay,
Whose memory in your immortality
Shall long outlast the Sun which gave them day.
Think how your essence differeth from theirs
In all but suffering! why partake
The agony to which they must be heirs—
Born to be ploughed with years, and sown with cares,
And reaped by Death, lord of the human soil?
Even had their days been left to toil their path
Through time to dust, unshortened by God's wrath,
Still they are Evil's prey, and Sorrow's spoil.

AHOLIBAMAH - Let them fly!
I hear the voice which says that all must die,
Sooner than our white-bearded patriarchs died;
And that on high
An ocean is prepared,
While from below
The deep shall rise to meet Heaven's overflow—
Few shall be spared,
It seems; and, of that few, the race of Cain
Must lift their eyes to Adam's God in vain.
Sister! since it is so,
And the eternal Lord
In vain would be implored

For the remission of one hour of woe,
Let us resign even what we have adored,
And meet the wave, as we would meet the sword,
If not unmoved, yet undismayed,
And wailing less for us than those who shall
Survive in mortal or immortal thrall,
And, when the fatal waters are allayed,
Weep for the myriads who can weep no more.
Fly, Seraphs! to your own eternal shore,
Where winds nor howl, nor waters roar.
Our portion is to die,
And yours to live for ever:
But which is best, a dead Eternity,
Or living, is but known to the great Giver.
Obey him, as we shall obey;
I would not keep this life of mine in clay
An hour beyond his will;
Nor see ye lose a portion of his grace,
For all the mercy which Seth's race

Find still.
Fly!
And as your pinions bear ye back to Heaven,
Think that my love still mounts with thee on high,
Samiasa!
And if I look up with a tearless eye,
'Tis that an angel's bride disdains to weep,—
Farewell! Now rise, inexorable deep!

ANAH - And must we die?
And must I lose thee too,
Azaziel?
Oh, my heart! my heart!
Thy prophecies were true!
And yet thou wert so happy too!
The blow, though not unlooked for, falls as new:
But yet depart!
Ah! why?
Yet let me not retain thee—fly!
My pangs can be but brief; but thine would be
Eternal, if repulsed from Heaven for me.
Too much already hast thou deigned
To one of Adam's race!

Our doom is sorrow: not to us alone,
But to the Spirits who have not disdained
To love us, cometh anguish with disgrace.
The first who taught us knowledge hath been hurled
From his once archangelic throne
Into some unknown world:
And thou, Azaziel! No—
Thou shalt not suffer woe
For me. Away! nor weep!
Thou canst not weep; but yet
May'st suffer more, not weeping: then forget
Her, whom the surges of the all-strangling deep
Can bring no pang like this. Fly! fly!
Being gone, 'twill be less difficult to die.

JAPHET - Oh say not so!
Father! and thou, archangel, thou!
Surely celestial mercy lurks below
That pure severe serenity of brow:
Let them not meet this sea without a shore,
Save in our ark, or let me be no more!

NOAH - Peace, child of passion, peace!
If not within thy heart, yet with thy tongue
Do God no wrong!
Live as he wills it—die, when he ordains,
A righteous death, unlike the seed of Cain's.

Cease, or be sorrowful in silence; cease
To weary Heaven's ear with thy selfish plaint.
Wouldst thou have God commit a sin for thee?
Such would it be
To alter his intent
For a mere mortal sorrow. Be a man!
And bear what Adam's race must bear, and can.

JAPHET - Aye, father! but when they are gone,
And we are all alone,
Floating upon the azure desert, and
The depth beneath us hides our own dear land,
And dearer, silent friends and brethren, all
Buried in its immeasurable breast,
Who, who, our tears, our shrieks, shall then command?
Can we in Desolation's peace have rest?
Oh God! be thou a God, and spare
Yet while 'tis time!
Renew not Adam's fall:
Mankind were then but twain,
But they are numerous now as are the waves
And the tremendous rain,
Whose drops shall be less thick than would their graves,
Were graves permitted to the seed of Cain.

NOAH - Silence, vain boy! each word of thine's a crime.
Angel! forgive this stripling's fond despair.

RAPHAEL - Seraphs! these mortals speak in passion: Ye!
Who are, or should be, passionless and pure,
May now return with me.

SAMIASA - It may not be:
We have chosen, and will endure.

RAPHAEL - Say'st thou?

AZAZIEL - He hath said it, and I say, Amen!

RAPHAEL - Again!
Then from this hour,
Shorn as ye are of all celestial power,
And aliens from your God,
Farewell!

JAPHET - Alas! where shall they dwell?
Hark, hark! Deep sounds, and deeper still,
Are howling from the mountain's bosom:
There's not a breath of wind upon the hill,
Yet quivers every leaf, and drops each blossom:
Earth groans as if beneath a heavy load.

NOAH - Hark, hark! the sea-birds cry!
In clouds they overspread the lurid sky,
And hover round the mountain, where before
Never a white wing, wetted by the wave,
Yet dared to soar,
Even when the waters waxed too fierce to brave.
Soon it shall be their only shore,
And then, no more!

JAPHET - The sun! the sun!
He riseth, but his better light is gone;
And a black circle, bound
His glaring disk around,
Proclaims Earth's last of summer days hath shone!

The clouds return into the hues of night,
Save where their brazen-coloured edges streak
The verge where brighter morns were wont to break.

NOAH - And lo! yon flash of light,
The distant thunder's harbinger, appears!
It cometh! hence, away!
Leave to the elements their evil prey!
Hence to where our all-hallowed ark uprears
Its safe and wreckless sides!

JAPHET - Oh, father, stay!
Leave not my Anah to the swallowing tides!

NOAH - Must we not leave all life to such? Begone!

JAPHET - Not I.

NOAH - Then die
With them!
How darest thou look on that prophetic sky,
And seek to save what all things now condemn,
In overwhelming unison
With just Jehovah's wrath!

JAPHET - Can rage and justice join in the same path?

NOAH - Blasphemer! darest thou murmur even now!

RAPHAEL - Patriarch, be still a father! smooth thy brow:
Thy son, despite his folly, shall not sink:
He knows not what he says, yet shall not drink
With sobs the salt foam of the swelling waters;
But be, when passion passeth, good as thou,
Nor perish like Heaven's children with man's daughters.

AHOLIBAMAH - The tempest cometh; heaven and earth unite
For the annihilation of all life.
Unequal is the strife
Between our strength and the Eternal Might!

SAMIASA - But ours is with thee; we will bear ye far
To some untroubled star,
Where thou, and Anah, shalt partake our lot:
And if thou dost not weep for thy lost earth,
Our forfeit Heaven shall also be forgot.

ANAH - Oh! my dear father's tents, my place of birth,
And mountains, land, and woods! when ye are not,
Who shall dry up my tears?

AZAZIEL - Thy spirit-lord.
Fear not; though we are shut from Heaven,
Yet much is ours, whence we can not be driven.

RAPHAEL - Rebel! thy words are wicked, as thy deeds
Shall henceforth be but weak: the flaming sword,
Which chased the first-born out of Paradise,
Still flashes in the angelic hands.

AZAZIEL - It cannot slay us: threaten dust with death,
And talk of weapons unto that which bleeds.
What are thy swords in our immortal eyes?

RAPHAEL - The moment cometh to approve thy strength;
And learn at length
How vain to war with what thy God commands:
Thy former force was in thy faith.

Enter MORTALS, flying for refuge.

Chorus of MORTALS - The heavens and earth are mingling—God! oh God!
What have we done? Yet spare!
Hark! even the forest beasts howl forth their prayer!
The dragon crawls from out his den,
To herd, in terror, innocent with men;
And the birds scream their agony through air.
Yet, yet, Jehovah! yet withdraw thy rod
Of wrath, and pity thine own world's despair!
Hear not man only but all nature plead!

RAPHAEL - Farewell, thou earth! ye wretched sons of clay,
I cannot, must not, aid you. 'Tis decreed!

[Exit RAPHAEL

JAPHET - Some clouds sweep on as vultures for their prey,
While others, fixed as rocks, await the word
At which their wrathful vials shall be poured.
No azure more shall robe the firmament,
Nor spangled stars be glorious: Death hath risen:
In the Sun's place a pale and ghastly glare
Hath wound itself around the dying air.

AZAZIEL - Come, Anah! quit this chaos-founded prison,
To which the elements again repair,
To turn it into what it was: beneath
The shelter of these wings thou shalt be safe,
As was the eagle's nestling once within
Its mother's.—Let the coming chaos chafe

With all its elements! Heed not their din!
A brighter world than this, where thou shalt breathe
Ethereal life, will we explore:
These darkened clouds are not the only skies.

[AZAZIEL and SAMIASA fly off, and disappear with ANAH and AHOLIBAMAH.

JAPHET - They are gone! They have disappeared amidst the roar
Of the forsaken world; and never more,
Whether they live, or die with all Earth's life,
Now near its last, can aught restore
Anah unto these eyes.

Chorus of MORTALS - Oh son of Noah! mercy on thy kind!
What! wilt thou leave us all—all—all behind?
While safe amidst the elemental strife,
Thou sitt'st within thy guarded ark?
A Mother (offering her infant to Japhet).
Oh, let this child embark!
I brought him forth in woe,
But thought it joy
To see him to my bosom clinging so.
Why was he born?
What hath he done—
My unweaned son—
To move Jehovah's wrath or scorn?
What is there in this milk of mine, that Death
Should stir all Heaven and Earth up to destroy
My boy,
And roll the waters o'er his placid breath?
Save him, thou seed of Seth!
Or curséd be—with him who made
Thee and thy race, for which we are betrayed!

JAPHET - Peace! 'tis no hour for curses, but for prayer!

Chorus of MORTALS - For prayer!!!
And where
Shall prayer ascend,
When the swoln clouds unto the mountains bend
And burst,
And gushing oceans every barrier rend,
Until the very deserts know no thirst?
Accursed
Be he who made thee and thy sire!
We deem our curses vain; we must expire;
But as we know the worst,
Why should our hymns be raised, our knees be bent
Before the implacable Omnipotent,
Since we must fall the same?
If he hath made Earth, let it be his shame,
To make a world for torture.—Lo! they come,
The loathsome waters, in their rage!
And with their roar make wholesome nature dumb!
The forest's trees (coeval with the hour
When Paradise upsprung,
Ere Eve gave Adam knowledge for her dower,
Or Adam his first hymn of slavery sung),
So massy, vast, yet green in their old age,
Are overtopped,
Their summer blossoms by the surges lopped,
Which rise, and rise, and rise.
Vainly we look up to the lowering skies—
They meet the seas,
And shut out God from our beseeching eyes.
Fly, son of Noah, fly! and take thine ease,
In thine allotted ocean-tent;
And view, all floating o'er the element,
The corpses of the world of thy young days:
Then to Jehovah raise
Thy song of praise!
A MORTAL - Blesséd are the dead
Who die in the Lord!
And though the waters be o'er earth outspread,
Yet, as his word,
Be the decree adored!
He gave me life—he taketh but
The breath which is his own:
And though these eyes should be for ever shut,

Nor longer this weak voice before his throne
Be heard in supplicating tone,
Still blesséd be the Lord,
For what is past,
For that which is:
For all are his,
From first to last—

Time—Space—Eternity—Life—Death—
The vast known and immeasurable unknown.
He made, and can unmake;
And shall
I, for a little gasp of breath,
Blaspheme and groan?
No; let me die, as I have lived, in faith,
Nor quiver, though the Universe may quake!

Chorus of MORTALS - Where shall we fly?
Not to the mountains high;
For now their torrents rush, with double roar,
To meet the Ocean, which, advancing still,
Already grasps each drowning hill,
Nor leaves an unsearched cave.
Enter a Woman. Woman.
Oh, save me, save!
Our valley is no more:
My father and my father's tent,
My brethren and my brethren's herds,
The pleasant trees that o'er our noonday bent,
And sent forth evening songs from sweetest birds,
The little rivulet which freshened all
Our pastures green,
No more are to be seen.
When to the mountain cliff I climbed this morn,
I turned to bless the spot,
And not a leaf appeared about to fall;—
And now they are not!—
Why was I born?

JAPHET - To die! in youth to die!
And happier in that doom,
Than to behold the universal tomb,
Which I
Am thus condemned to weep above in vain.
Why, when all perish, why must I remain?

[The waters rise; MEN fly in every direction; many are overtaken by the waves: the Chorus of
MORTALS disperses in search of safety up the mountains: JAPHET remains upon a rock, while the Ark
floats towards him in the distance.

Lord Byron – A Short Biography

Byron, one of England's greatest poets, endured a quite difficult background. His father, Captain
John "Mad Jack" Byron had married his second wife, the former Catherine Gordon, a descendant of
Cardinal Beaton and heiress of the Gight estate in Aberdeenshire, Scotland for the same reason that
he married his first: her money. Byron's mother-to-be had to sell her land and title to pay her new
husband's debts and within two years the large estate of £23,500, had been squandered, leaving her
with an annual income in trust of £150. In a move to avoid his creditors, Catherine accompanied her

husband to France in 1786, but returned to England at the end of 1787 in order to give birth to her son on English soil.

George Gordon Byron was born on January 22nd 1788, in lodgings, at Holles Street in London although there is a conflicting account of him having been born in Dover.

He was christened, at St Marylebone Parish Church, George Gordon Byron, after his maternal grandfather, George Gordon of Gight, a descendant of James I of Scotland, who, in 1779, had committed suicide.

In 1790 Catherine moved back to Aberdeenshire and it was here that Byron spent his childhood. His father joined them in their lodgings in Queen Street, but the couple quickly separated. Catherine was prone to mood swings and melancholy. Her husband continued to borrow money from her and she fell deeper into debt. It was one of these "loans" that allowed him to travel to Valenciennes, France, where he died in 1791.

When Byron's great-uncle, the "wicked" Lord Byron, died on 21 May 1798, the 10-year-old boy became the 6th Baron Byron of Rochdale and inherited the ancestral home, Newstead Abbey, in Nottinghamshire. However the Abbey was in a state of disrepair and it was leased to Lord Grey de Ruthyn, and others for several years.

Catherine's parenting swung between either spoiling or indulging her son to stubbornly refusing every plea. Her drinking disgusted him, and he mocked her short and corpulent frame. She did retaliate and, in a fit of temper, once called him as "a lame brat", on account of his club-foot, an issue on which we was very sensitive. He referred to himself as "le diable boiteux" ("the limping devil").

Byron early education was taken at Aberdeen Grammar School, and in August 1799 he entered the school of Dr. William Glennie, in Dulwich. He was encouraged to exercise in moderation but could not restrain himself from "violent" bouts in an attempt to overcompensate for his deformed foot. His mother interfered, often withdrawing him from school, and resulting in him lacking discipline and neglecting his classical studies.

In 1801 he was sent to Harrow, where he remained until July 1805. Byron was an excellent orator but undistinguished student and an unskilled cricketer but strangely he did represent the school in the very first Eton v Harrow cricket match at Lord's in 1805.

Byron, always prone to over-indulge, fell in love with Mary Chaworth, whom he met while at school, and thence refused to return to Harrow in September 1803. His mother wrote, "He has no indisposition that I know of but love, desperate love, the worst of all maladies in my opinion. In short, the boy is distractedly in love with Miss Chaworth."

He did finally return in January 1804, and described his friends there; "My school friendships were with me passions for I was always violent." His nostalgic poems about his Harrow friendships, in his book Childish Recollections, published in 1806, talk of a "consciousness of sexual differences that may in the end make England untenable to him".

The following autumn he attended Trinity College, Cambridge, where he met and formed a close bond with John Edleston. On his "protégé" Byron wrote, "He has been my almost constant associate since October, 1805, when I entered Trinity College. His voice first attracted my attention, his countenance fixed it, and his manners attached me to him forever." In his memory Byron composed

Thyrza, a series of elegies. In later years Byron described the affair as "a violent, though pure love and passion". The public were beginning to view homosexuality with increasing distaste and the law now specified such sanctions as public hanging against convicted or even suspected offenders. Though equally Byron may just be using 'pure' out of respect for Edleston's innocence, in contrast to the more sexually overt relations experienced at Harrow School. Byron is now thought of as bi-sexual though more fulfilled, on all levels, by women.

While not at school or college, Byron lived with his mother in Southwell, Nottinghamshire. While there, he cultivated friendships with Elizabeth Pigot and her brother, John, with whom he staged two plays for the entertainment of the local community. During this time, with the help of Elizabeth, who copied his rough drafts, he wrote his first volumes of poetry, Fugitive Pieces, which included poems written when Byron was only 14. However, it was promptly recalled and burned on the advice of his friend, the Reverend J. T. Becher, on account of its more amorous verses, particularly the poem To Mary.

Hours of Idleness, which collected many of the previous poems, along with recent compositions, was the culminating book. The savage, anonymous criticism this received in the Edinburgh Review prompted his first major satire, English Bards and Scotch Reviewers in 1809. This was put into the hands of his relative, R. C. Dallas, requesting him to "...get it published without his name". Although published anonymously Byron was generally known to be the author. The work so upset some of his critics they challenged Byron to a duel. Of course, over time, it became a mark of renown to be the target of Byron's pen.

Byron first took his seat in the House of Lords March 13th, 1809. He was a strong advocate of social reform, and one of the few Parliamentary defenders of the Luddites: specifically, he was against a death penalty for Luddite "frame breakers" in Nottinghamshire, who destroyed the textile machines that were putting them out of work. His first speech before the Lords, on February 27th, 1812, sarcastically referenced the "benefits" of automation, which he saw as producing inferior material as well as putting people out of work, and concluded the proposed law was only missing two things to be effective: "Twelve Butchers for a Jury and a Jeffries for a Judge!"

Two months later, Byron made another impassioned speech before the House in support of Catholic emancipation. He expressed opposition to the established religion because it was unfair to people who practiced other faiths.

Out of this period would follow several overtly political poems; Song for the Luddites (1816), The Landlords' Interest, Canto XIV of The Age of Bronze, Wellington: The Best of the Cut-Throats (1819) and The Intellectual Eunuch Castlereagh (1818).

Like his father Byron racked up numerous debts. His mother thought he had "reckless disregard for money" and lived in fear of her son's creditors.

Between1809 to 1811, Byron went on the Grand Tour, then customary for a young nobleman. The Napoleonic Wars meant most of Europe had to be avoided, and he instead ventured south to the Mediterranean.

There is some correspondence among his circle of Cambridge friends that suggests that another motive was the hope of homosexual experience, and other theories saying that he was worried about a possible dalliance with a married woman, Mary Chaworth, his former love.

But other possibilities exist. Byron had read much about the Ottoman and Persian lands as a child, was attracted to Islam (especially Sufi mysticism), and later wrote, "With these countries, and events connected with them, all my really poetical feelings begin and end."

Byron began his trip in Portugal from where he wrote a letter to his friend Mr. Hodgson in which he describes his mastery of the Portuguese language, consisting mainly of swearing and insults. Byron particularly enjoyed his stay in Sintra that is described in Childe Harold's Pilgrimage as "glorious Eden". From Lisbon he travelled overland to Seville, Jerez de la Frontera, Cádiz, Gibraltar and from there by sea on to Malta and Greece.

While in Athens, Byron met 14-year-old Nicolò Giraud, who became quite close and taught him Italian. Byron sent Giraud to school at a monastery in Malta and in his will, though later taken out, bequeathed him a sizeable sum.

Byron then moved on to Smyrna, and then Constantinople on board HMS Salsette. While HMS Salsette was anchored awaiting Ottoman permission to dock at the city, on May 3rd, 1810 Byron and Lieutenant Ekenhead, of Salsette 's Marines, swam the Hellespont. Byron commemorated this feat in the second canto of Don Juan.

When he sailed back to England in April 1811, he travelled, for a time, aboard the transport ship Hydra, which had on board the last large shipments of Lord Elgin's marbles, a piece of vandalism that Byron had longed railed against. The last leg of his voyage home was from Malta in aboard HMS Volage. He arrived at Sheerness, Kent, on July 14$^{th.}$ He was home after two years away.

On August 2nd, his mother died. "I had but one friend in the world," he exclaimed, "and she is gone."

The following year, 1812, Byron became a sensation with the publication, via his literary agent and family relative R. C. Dallas, of the first two cantos of 'Childe Harold's Pilgrimage'. He rapidly became the most brilliant star in the dazzling world of Regency London, sought after at every society venue, elected to several exclusive clubs, and frequented the most fashionable London drawing-rooms. His own words recall; "I awoke one morning and found myself famous". The Edinburgh Review allowed that Byron had "improved marvellously since his last appearance at our tribunal." He followed up his success with the poem's last two cantos, as well as four equally celebrated "Oriental Tales": The Giaour, The Bride of Abydos, The Corsair and Lara.

His affair with Lady Caroline Lamb (who called him "mad, bad and dangerous to know"), as well as other women and the constant pressure of debt, caused him to seek a suitable marriage i.e. marry wealth. One choice was Annabella Milbanke. But in 1813 he met again, after four years, his half-sister, Augusta Leigh. Rumours of incest constantly surrounded the pair; Augusta, who was married, gave birth on April 15th, 1814 to her third daughter, Elizabeth Medora Leigh, and Byron is suspected to be the father.

To escape from debts and rumours he now sought, in earnest, to marry Annabella, (said to be the likely heiress of a rich uncle). They married on January 2nd, 1815, and their daughter, Ada, was born in December of that year. However Byron's continuing obsession with Augusta and dalliances with others made their marriage a misery.

Annabella thought Byron insane and she left him, taking Ada, in January 1816 and began proceedings for a legal separation. For Byron the scandal of the separation, the continuing rumours about Augusta, and ever-increasing debts were to now force him to leave England.

He passed through Belgium and along the river Rhine and by the summer was settled at the Villa Diodati by Lake Geneva, Switzerland, with his personal physician, the young, brilliant, and handsome John William Polidori. There Byron befriended the poet Percy Bysshe Shelley, and his future wife Mary Godwin. He was also joined by Mary's stepsister, Claire Clairmont, with whom, almost inevitably, he had had an affair with in London.

Kept indoors at the Villa Diodati by the incessant rain during three days in June, the five turned to writing. Mary Shelley produced what would become Frankenstein, or The Modern Prometheus, and Polidori was inspired by a fragmentary story of Byron's, Fragment of a Novel, to produce The Vampyre, the progenitor of the romantic vampire genre.

Byron's story fragment was published as a postscript to Mazeppa; he also now wrote the third canto of Childe Harold.

Byron wintered in Venice, pausing his travels when he fell in love with Marianna Segati, in whose Venice house he was lodging, but who was soon replaced by 22-year-old Margarita Cogni; both women were married. Cogni, who could not read or write, left her husband to move into Byron's Venice house. Their fighting often caused Byron to spend nights in his gondola; when he asked her to leave the house, she threw herself into the Venetian canal.

In a visit to San Lazzaro degli Armeni in Venice, he began to immerse himself in Armenian culture. He learned the Armenian language, and attended many seminars about language and history. He co-authored English Grammar and Armenian in 1817, and Armenian Grammar and English in 1819, where he included quotations from classical and modern Armenian and later, in 1821, participated in the compilation of the English Armenian dictionary, and in the preface he mapped out the relationship of the Armenians with, and the oppression of, the Turkish "pashas" and the Persian satraps, and their struggle for liberation.

In 1817 after a visit to Rome and back in Venice, he wrote the fourth canto of Childe Harold and sold his ancestral home, Newstead Abbey, as well as publishing Manfred; A Dramatic Poem and , Cain; A Mystery.

Byron wrote the first five cantos of his renowned Don Juan between 1818 and 1820. And besides work and adventure there was always love. Women, of course, were always in evidence and the young Countess Teresa Guiccioli found her first love in Byron, who in turn asked her to elope with him. They lived in Ravenna between 1819 and 1821 where he continued Don Juan and also wrote the Ravenna Diary, My Dictionary and Recollections.

It was here that he now received visits from Percy Bysshe Shelley and Thomas Moore.

Of Byron's lifestyle in Ravenna Shelley informs us that; "Lord Byron gets up at two. I get up, quite contrary to my usual custom … at 12. After breakfast we sit talking till six. From six to eight we gallop through the pine forest which divide Ravenna from the sea; we then come home and dine, and sit up gossiping till six in the morning. I don't suppose this will kill me in a week or fortnight, but I shall not try it longer. Lord B.'s establishment consists, besides servants, of ten horses, eight enormous dogs, three monkeys, five cats, an eagle, a crow, and a falcon; and all these, except the horses, walk about the house, which every now and then resounds with their unarbitrated quarrels, as if they were the masters of it… . [P.S.] I find that my enumeration of the animals in this Circean Palace was defective …. I have just met on the grand staircase five peacocks, two guinea hens, and an Egyptian crane. I wonder who all these animals were before they were changed into these shapes."

From 1821 to 1822, he finished Cantos 6–12 of Don Juan at Pisa, and in the same year he joined with Leigh Hunt and Percy Bysshe Shelley in starting a short-lived newspaper, The Liberal, in the first number of which appeared The Vision of Judgment.

For the first time since his arrival in Italy, Byron found himself tempted to give dinner parties; his guests included the Shelleys, Edward Ellerker Williams, Thomas Medwin, John Taaffe and Edward John Trelawney; and "never", as Shelley said, "did he display himself to more advantage than on these occasions; being at once polite and cordial, full of social hilarity and the most perfect good humour; never diverging into ungraceful merriment, and yet keeping up the spirit of liveliness throughout the evening."

Byron's mother-in-law Judith Noel, the Hon. Lady Milbanke, died in 1822. Her will required that he change his surname to "Noel" in order for him to inherit half of her estate. He obtained a Royal Warrant allowing him to "take and use the surname of Noel only". The Royal Warrant also allowed him to "subscribe the said surname of Noel before all titles of honour", and from that point he signed himself "Noel Byron" (the usual signature of a peer being merely the peerage, in this case simply "Byron").

The Shelley's and Williams had rented a house on the coast and had a schooner built. Byron decided that he too should have his own yacht, and engaged Trelawny's friend, Captain Daniel Roberts, to design and construct the boat. It was named the Bolivar.

On July 8th, 1822 Shelley drowned in a boating accident. Byron attended the funeral. Shelley was cremated on the beach at Viareggio where his body had washed up. His ashes were later interred in Rome in the cemetery in Rome where lay already his son William and John Keats.

Byron was living in Genoa when, in 1823, while growing bored, he accepted a call for his help from representatives of the movement for Greek independence from the Ottoman Empire. With the assistance of his banker and Captain Daniel Roberts, Byron chartered the Brig Hercules to take him to Greece. On 16 July, Byron left Genoa arriving at Kefalonia in the Ionian Islands on August 4th.

Byron had spent £4,000 of his own money to refit the Greek fleet and sailed for Missolonghi in western Greece, arriving on December 29th, to join Alexandros Mavrokordatos, a Greek politician with military power. When the famous Danish sculptor Bertel Thorvaldsen heard about Byron's heroics in Greece, he voluntarily re-sculpted his earlier bust of Byron in Greek marble.

Mavrokordatos and Byron planned to attack the Turkish-held fortress of Lepanto, at the mouth of the Gulf of Corinth. Byron employed a fire-master to prepare artillery and took part of the rebel army under his own command, despite his lack of military experience. Before the expedition could sail, on February 15th, 1824, he fell ill, and the usual remedy of bloodletting weakened him further. He made a partial recovery, but in early April he caught a violent cold which further therapeutic bleeding, insisted on by his doctors, aggravated. He developed a violent fever, and died in Missolonghi on April 19th.

Alfred, Lord Tennyson would later recall the shocked reaction in Britain when word was received of Byron's death. The Greeks mourned Lord Byron deeply, and he became a hero. The Greek form of "Byron", continues in popularity as a name in Greece, and a town near Athens is called Vyronas in his honour.

Byron's body was embalmed, but the Greeks wanted their hero to stay with them. Some say his heart was removed to remain in Missolonghi. His body was returned to England (despite his dying wishes that it should not) for burial in Westminster Abbey, but the Abbey refused to accept it on the grounds of "questionable morality".

Huge crowds viewed his body as he lay in state for two days in London before being buried at the Church of St. Mary Magdalene in Hucknall, Nottinghamshire. A marble slab given by the King of Greece is laid directly above Byron's grave.

Byron's friends had raised the sum of £1,000 to commission a statue of the writer by the sculptor Thorvaldsen. However for a decade after the statue was completed, in 1834, most British institutions had refused to accept it, among them the British Museum, St. Paul's Cathedral, Westminster Abbey and the National Gallery, and it remained in storage. Finally Trinity College, Cambridge, placed the statue in its library.

Finally, in 1969, a145 years after Byron's death, a memorial to him was placed in Westminster Abbey. It had been pointedly noted by the New York Times that "People are beginning to ask whether this ignoring of Byron is not a thing of which England should be ashamed ... a bust or a tablet might be put in the Poets' Corner and England be relieved of ingratitude toward one of her really great sons." At last Byron was where he should be.

Lord Byron – A Concise Bibliography

The Major Works
Hours of Idleness (1807)
English Bards and Scotch Reviewers (1809)
Childe Harold's Pilgrimage, Cantos I & II (1812)
The Giaour (1813)
The Bride of Abydos (1813)
The Corsair (1814)
Lara, A Tale (1814)
Hebrew Melodies (1815)
The Siege of Corinth (1816)
Parisina (1816)
The Prisoner of Chillon (1816)
The Dream (1816)
Prometheus (1816)
Darkness (1816)
Manfred (1817)
The Lament of Tasso (1817)
Beppo (1818)
Childe Harold's Pilgrimage (1818)
Don Juan (1819–1824; incomplete on Byron's death in 1824)
Mazeppa (1819)
The Prophecy of Dante (1819)
Marino Faliero (1820)
Sardanapalus (1821)
The Two Foscari (1821)
Cain (1821)
The Vision of Judgment (1821)
Heaven and Earth (1821)

Werner (1822)
The Age of Bronze (1823)
The Island (1823)
The Deformed Transformed (1824)

Darkness
The Death of Calmar and Orla
The Deformed Transformed, a drama (A transcription project)
The Destruction of Sennacherib
The Devil's Drive
Don Juan
A Dream (same as "Darkness")
The Dream
The Duel

E

E Nihilo Nihil; or, An Epigram Bewitched
Egotism. A Letter to J. T. Becher
Elegiac Stanzas on the Death of Sir Peter Parker, Bart.
Elegy
Elegy on Newstead Abbey
Elegy on the Death of Sir Peter Parker (same "Elegiac Stanzas on the Death of Sir Peter Parker, Bart.")
Endorsement to the Deed of Separation, in the April of 1816
English Bards, and Scotch Reviewers, a Satire
Epigram (If for Silver, or for Gold)
Epigram (In Digging up your Bones, Tom Paine)
Epigram (It Seems That the Braziers Propose Soon to Pass)
Epigram (The world is a bundle of hay)
Epigram on an Old Lady Who Had Some Curious Notions Respecting the Soul
Epigrams (Oh, Castlereagh! Thou Art a Patriot Now)
Epilogue
The Episode of Nisus and Euryalus (A Paraphrase from the Æneid, Lib. 9.)
Epistle from Mr. Murray to Dr. Polidori
Epistle to a Friend
Epistle to Augusta
Epistle to Mr. Murray
Epitaph
Epitaph for Joseph Blacket, Late Poet and Shoemaker
Epitaph for William Pitt
Epitaph on a Beloved Friend
Epitaph on a Friend (same as "Epitaph on a Beloved Friend")
Epitaph on John Adams, of Southwell
Epitaph to a Dog
Euthanasia

F

Fame, Wisdom, Love, and Power Were Mine (same as "All is Vanity, saith the Preacher")
Fare Thee Well
Farewell (same as "Farewell! if Ever Fondest Prayer")
Farewell Petition to J. C. H., Esqre.
Farewell to Malta
Farewell to the Muse
Fill the Goblet Again
The First Kiss of Love
A Fragment (Could I Remount the River of My Years)
Fragment (Hills of Annesley, Bleak and Barren)

A Fragment (When, to Their Airy Hall, my Fathers' Voice)
Fragment from the "Monk of Athos"
Fragment of a Translation from the 9th Book of Virgil's Æneid (compare "The Episode of Nisus and Euryalus")
Fragment of an Epistle to Thomas Moore
Fragments of School Exercises: From the "Prometheus Vinctus" of Æschylus
Francesca of Rimini
Francisca
From Anacreon Ode 3. ('Twas Now the Hour When Night Had Driven)
From Job (same as "A Spirit Passed Before Me")
From the French (Ægle, Beauty and Poet, Has Two Little Crimes)
From the French (Must Thou Go, my Glorious Chief)
From the Last Hill That Looks on Thy Once Holy Dome (same as "On the Day of the Destruction of Jerusalem by Titus")
From the Portuguese
From the Turkish (same as "The Chain I Gave")

G

G. G. B. to E. P. (same as "To M. S. G.") (When I Dream That You Love Me, you'll surely Forgive)
The Giaour
The Girl of Cadiz
Granta. A Medley

H

The Harp the Monarch Minstrel Swept
Heaven and Earth, a Mystery (A transcription project)
Hebrew Melodies
Herod's Lament for Mariamne
Hints from Horace (A transcription project)
Hours of Idleness

I

I Speak Not, I Trace Not, I Breathe Not Thy Name (see "Stanzas for Music")
I Saw Thee Weep
I Would I Were a Careless Child
Ich Dien
If Sometimes in the Haunts of Men
If That High World
Imitated from Catullus
Imitation of Tibullus
Impromptu
Impromptu, in Reply to a Friend
In the Valley of Waters (same as "By the Waters of Babylon")
Inscription on the Monument of a Newfoundland Dog
The Island, or Christian and His Comrades
The Irish Avatar
It is the Hour (compare with first stanza of Parisina)

J

Jeptha's Daughter
John Keats

Journal in Cephalonia
Julian [a Fragment]

K

L
La Revanche
Lachin y Gair
L'Amitié est L'Amour sans Ailes
The Lament of Tasso
Lara: A Tale
Last Words on Greece
Lines Addressed by Lord Byron to Mr. Hobhouse on his Election for Westminster
Lines Addressed to a Young Lady
Lines Addressed to the Rev. J. T. Becher
Lines Inscribed Upon a Cup Formed From a Skull
Lines in the Travellers' Book at Orchomenus
Lines on Hearing That Lady Byron Was Ill
Lines on Sir Peter Parker (same as "Elegiac Stanzas on the Death of Sir Peter Parker, Bart.")
Lines to a Lady Weeping (same as "To a Lady Weeping")
Lines to Mr. Hodgson
Lines Written Beneath a Picture
Lines Written Beneath an Elm in the Churchyard of Harrow
Lines Written in an Album, At Malta
Lines Written in "Letters of an Italian Nun and an English Gentleman
Lines Written on a Blank Leaf of The Pleasures of Memory
Lord Byron's Verses on Sam Rogers
Love and Death
Love and Gold
A Love Song. To — (same as "Remind me not, Remind me not")
Love's Last Adieu
Lucietta. A Fragment

M
Maid of Athens, Ere We Part
Manfred, a Dramatic Poem
Marino Faliero, Doge of Venice, an Historical Tragedy (1821) (A transcription project)
Martial, Lib. I. Epig. I.
Mazeppa
Monody on the Death of the Right Hon. R. B. Sheridan
The Morgante Maggiore (A transcription project)
My Boy Hobbie O
My Epitaph
My Soul is Dark

N
Napoleon's Farewell
Napoleon's Snuff-box
The New Vicar of Bray
Newstead Abbey

Queries to Casuists

R
R. C. Dallas
Remember Him, whom Passion's Power
Remember Thee! Remember thee!
Remembrance
Remind Me Not, Remind Me Not
Reply to Some Verses of J. M. B. Pigot, Esq., on the Cruelty of his Mistress

S
Sardanapalus, a Tragedy (A transcription project)
Saul
She Walks in Beauty
The Siege of Corinth
A Sketch From Life
So We'll Go No More A-Roving
Soliloquy of a Bard in the Country
Sonetto di Vittorelli
Song (Breeze of the Night in Gentler Sighs)
Song (Fill the Goblet Again! For I Never Before)
Song (Maid of Athens, Ere We Part) (same as "Maid of Athens, Ere We Part")
Song (Thou Art Not False, But Thou Art fickle) same as "Thou Art Not False, But Thou Art Fickle")
Song (When I Roved a Young Highlander) (same as "When I Roved a Young Highlander")
Song For the Luddites
Song of Saul Before His Last Battle
Song To the Suliotes
Sonnet On Chillon
Sonnet on the Nuptials of the Marquis Antonio Cavalli with the Countess Clelia Rasponi of Ravenna
Sonnet, to Genevra (Thine eyes' Blue Tenderness, Thy Long Fair Hair)
Sonnet, to Generva (Thy Cheek is Pale with Thought, but Not From Woe). aka "Sonnet, to the Same"
Sonnet to Lake Leman
Sonnet to the Prince Regent
The Spell is Broke, the Charm is Flown!
A Spirit Passed Before Me
Stanzas (And Thou Art Dead, as Young and Fair)
Stanzas (And Wilt Thou Weep When I am Low?) (same as "And Wilt Thou Weep When I Am Low?")
Stanzas (Away, Away, Ye Notes of Woe)
Stanzas (Chill and Mirk is the Nightly Blast) (same as "Stanzas Composed During a Thunderstorm")
Stanzas (Could Love For Ever)
Stanzas (I Would I Were a Careless Child) (same as "I Would I Were a Careless Child")
Stanzas (If Sometimes in the Haunts of Men)
Stanzas (One Struggle More, and I Am Free)
Stanzas (Remember Him, Whom Passion's Power)
Stanzas (Thou Art Not False, but Thou Art Fickle)
Stanzas (Through Cloudless Skies, in Silvery Sheen) (same as "Stanzas Written in Passing the Ambracian Gulf")
Stanzas (When a Man Hath No Freedom to Fight For at Home)
Stanzas Composed During a Thunderstorm
Stanzas For Music (Bright Be the Place of Thy Soul!)
Stanzas For Music (I Speak Not, I Trace Not, I Breathe Not Thy Name)

Stanzas For Music (There Be None of Beauty's Daughters)
Stanzas For Music (There's Not a Joy the World Can Give Like That it Takes Away)
Stanzas For Music (They Say That Hope is Happiness)
Stanzas To — (same as "Stanzas to Augusta": Though the Day of My Destiny's Over)
Stanzas To a Hindoo Air
Stanzas To a Lady, on Leaving England
Stanzas To a Lady, with the Poems of Camoëns
Stanzas To Augusta (When all around grew drear and dark)
Stanzas To Augusta (Though the day of my Destiny's over)
Stanzas To Jessy
Stanzas To the Po
Stanzas To the Same (same as "There was a Time, I need not name")
Stanzas Written in Passing the Ambracian Gulf
Stanzas Written on the Road Between Florence and Pisa
Substitute For an Epitaph
Sun of the Sleepless!
Sympathetic Address to a Young Lady (same as "Lines to a Lady Weeping")

T

The Tear
There Be None of Beauty's Daughters (see "Stanzas for Music")
There Was a Time, I Need Not Name
There's Not a Joy the World Can Give Like That it Takes Away (see "Stanzas for Music")
They say that Hope is Happiness (see "Stanzas for Music")
Thou Art Not False, but Thou Art Fickle
Thou Whose Spell Can Raise the Dead (same as "Saul")
Thoughts Suggested by a College Examination
Thy Days are Done
To — (But Once I Dared to Lift My Eyes)
To — (Oh! Well I Know Your Subtle Sex)
To A— (same as "To M—")
To a Beautiful Quaker
To a Knot of Ungenerous Critics
To a Lady (Oh! Had My Fate Been Join'd with Thine)
To a Lady (This Band, Which Bound Thy yellow Hair)
To a Lady (When Man, Expell'd from Eden's Bowers)
To a Lady Weeping (same as "Lines To a Lady Weeping")
To a Lady who Presented to the Author a Lock of Hair Braided with His Own, and Appointed a Night in December to Meet Him in the Garden
To a Vain Lady
To a Youthful Friend
To an Oak at Newstead
To Anne (Oh, Anne, Your Offences to Me Have Been Grievous)
To Anne (Oh Say Not, Sweet Anne, That the Fates Have Decreed)
To Belshazzar
To Caroline (Oh! When Shall the Grave Hide For Ever My Sorrow?)
To Caroline (Think'st thou I saw thy beauteous eyes)
To Caroline (When I Hear you Express an Affection so Warm)
To Caroline (You Say You Love, and Yet Your Eye)
To D—
To Dives. A Fragment

To E—
To Edward Noel Long, Esq.
To Eliza
To Emma
To E. N. L. Esq. (same as "To Edward Noel Long, Esq.")
To Florence
To George Anson Byron (?)
To George, Earl Delawarr
To Harriet
To Ianthe (The "Origin of Love!"—Ah, why) (same as "On Being Asked What Was the 'Origin of Love'")
To Ianthe (from Canto I of Childe Harold's Pilgrimage) (Not in Those Climes Where I Have Late Been Straying)
To Inez (from Canto I of Childe Harold's Pilgrimage) (Nay, Smile Not at My Sullen Brow)
To Julia (same as "To Lesbia!")
To Lesbia!
To Lord Thurlow
To M—
To Maria — (same as "To Emma")
To Mrs. — (same as "Well! Thou Art Happy")
To Mrs. Musters (same as "Stanzas To a Lady, On Leaving England")
To M. S. G. (When I Dream That You Love Me, You'll Surely Forgive)
To M. S. G. (Whene'er I View Those Lips of Thine)
To Marion
To Mary, on Receiving Her Picture
To Miss E. P. (same as "To Eliza")
To Mr. Murray (For Orford and for Waldegrave)
To Mr. Murray (Strahan, Tonson, Lintot of the Times)
To Mr. Murray (To Hook the Reader, You, John Murray)
To my Son
To Penelope
To Romance
To Samuel Rogers, Esq. (same as "Lines Written On a Blank Leaf of The Pleasures of Memory")
To Sir W. D. (same as "To a Youthful Friend")
To the Author of a Sonnet
To the Countess of Blessington
To the Duke of D— (same as "To the Duke of Dorset")
To the Duke of Dorset
To the Earl of — (same as "To the Earl of Clare")
To the Earl of Clare
To the Honble. Mrs. George Lamb
To the Prince Regent on the Repeal of the Bill of Attainder Against Lord E. Fitzgerald, June, 1819. (same as "Sonnet to the Prince Regent")
To the Rev. J. T. Becher (same as "Lines: Addressed to the Rev. J. T. Becher")
To the Same (same as "And Wilt Thou Weep When I Am Low?")
To the Sighing Strephon
To Thomas Moore (My Boat is on the Shore)
To Thomas Moore (Oh you, Who in all Names Can Tickle the Town)
To Thomas Moore (What Are You Doing Now)
To Thyrza (Without a Stone to Mark the Spot)
To Thyrza (One Struggle More, and I Am Free) (same as "One Struggle More, and I am Free")

To Time
To Woman
Translation from Anacreon Ode 1. (I Wish to Tune My Quivering Lyre)
Translation from Anacreon Ode 5. (Mingle with the Genial Bowl)
Translation from Catullus: Ad Lesbiam
Translation from Catullus: Lugete Veneres Cupidinesque
Translation from Horace
Translation from the "Medea" of Euripides [Ll. 627–660]
Translation from Vittorelli
Translation of a Romaic Love Song
Translation of the Epitaph on Virgil and Tibullus, by Domitius Marsus
Translation of the Famous Greek War Song
Translation of the Nurse's Dole in the Medea of Euripides
Translation of the Romaic Song
The Two Foscari, a Tragedy (A transcription project)

U

V
Venice. A Fragment
Verses Found in a Summer-house at Hales-Owen
Versicles
A Version of Ossian's Address to the Sun
A very Mournful Ballad on the Siege and Conquest of Alhama
Vision of Belshazzar
The Vision of Judgment (A transcription project)
A Volume of Nonsense

W
The Waltz, an Apostrophic Hymn
Warriors and Chiefs! (same as "Song of Saul Before His Last Battle")
We Sate Down and Wept by the Waters of Babel (same as "By the Rivers of Babylon We Sat Down and Wept")
Well! Thou art Happy
Were My Bosom as False as Thou Deem'st It To Be
Werner, or The Inheritance, a Tragedy (A transcription project)
When a Man Hath No Freedom to Fight For at Home (see "Stanzas")
When Coldness Wraps This Suffering Clay
When I Roved a Young Highlander
When We Two Parted
The Wild Gazelle
Windsor Poetics
A Woman's Hair
Written after Swimming from Sestos to Abydos
Written at Athens (same as "The Spell is Broke, the Charm is Flown!")
Written at the Request of a Lady in her Memorandum Book (same as "Lines Written in an Album, At Malta")
Written in an Album (same as "Lines Written in an Album, At Malta")
Written in Mrs. Spencer S.'s— (same as "Lines Written in an Album, At Malta")

www.ingramcontent.com/pod-product-compliance
Lightning Source LLC
Chambersburg PA
CBHW070112070426
42448CB00038B/2530